The ~~Sky is~~

NOT

the Limit!

A Book Of
Empowering Poetry

Alicea Crafter

*Priority*ONE
publications
Detroit, Michigan, USA

*Priority*ONE Publications
P. O. Box 725 • Farmington, MI 48332
(800) 331-8841 Nationwide Toll Free
E-mail: info@p1pubs.com
URL: http://www.p1pubs.com

ISBN 13: 978-1-933972-15-2
ISBN 10:   1-933972-15-7

Cover and interior paintings by Alicea Crafter

Edited by Paula Brinston and Nina Wheeler

Cover and interior design by PriorityONE Publications

Painting Photography by Sherwood Forest Art Gallery

Printed in the United States of America

*This book is devoted
to our spiritual empowerment.*

Table of Contents

Part One:
Infinite Possibilities

Infinite Possibilities by Alicea Crafter

This painting symbolizes the unlimited potential we can discover within ourselves.

Desire

We follow this drive
That lets us know we're alive.
Making us want to do more than just simply survive
Fueling our motivation to thrive.
It's this inner desire
That inspires us to go higher
though going further may not extinguish this fire.
Because we can always go on just a little bit more.
There will always be another unopened door.
And knowing that life's process
may never come to an end
Will cause some to stand still and others to begin again.

Dream Again

People what are you settling for?
Do you think you can acquire just a little bit more?
Some might be looking funny
Thinking that I'm just talking about money.
But this is about seeking knowledge.
And about someone starting or finishing college.
It's about that goal you have in you heart.
It may even be a business
that you've been wanting to start.
Is it false or is it true?
Do these things apply to you?
Now I know that some may be comfortable and content.
With just getting by paying the rent.
I know that some people just sit and pray.
Simply standing by, waiting on judgment day.
Just thought I should tell you that it's okay.
To make your trip on earth a more comfortable stay.
Sometime ago it was accepted
This lifestyle that was selected.
But as a child, what did you desire to be?
What was your vision? What did you see?
When was the day that you forfeited your fight?
You were free to dream but you gave up that right.
It doesn't matter what is the color of your skin
Or the neighborhood that you grew up in.
Your parents may have not been around.
Your family and friends may have put you down.
But you have the right to dream at night.
You have a future that is fruitful and bright!

Do you think that there's inside information
flowing outside of our community
And that the knowledge is controlled
while there is no sense of unity?
Well, even if there is truth in that
You still must consider this simple fact.
There is a brain inside of your head
With ideas for you to get ahead.
There is a heart inside of your chest.
Full of passion for you to be your best.
And there is a voice inside of your mouth
With positive words that have to come out.
And just as sure as you can blink
You have that right to dream and think.
No one on earth can give you the permission
To accept and complete your chosen mission.
The mission to fulfill your calling in life.
The mission to finally get this thing right.
There are wonderful plans for you.
But you have to believe in what you can do.
And you must do something!
Contribute and participate.
Use your powers that are mighty and great.
You can't lose hope! You can't lose sight!
You are free to dream and you must exercise that right.
Focus on the ability that you have within.
Enjoy your life and dream again.

Begin

How will we finish if we never start?
Will we know when things are together
if they have never fallen apart?
We will not reach our destination
nor our reward at the end
If we do not have in our hearts the courage to begin.
That's why I have decided that I will soar.
And that I will cherish my life even more.
After the ups and downs I've done the math.
I'm factoring in a different path.
Although I can not see my future, the light will lead me
My courage and understanding
will nourish and feed me.
And before I can walk through that brand new door
I must appreciate where I was before.
As I observe my history, I see a story.
It was investing in pain that earned my glory
Victory has always been mine. I even gain when I lose.
So no matter my weakness, going forward I will choose.
These journeys will last me my whole life long
I'm headed right to where I belong.
Although I am not sure what is in store at the end
One thing is for certain, I will begin.

At Night

When it is hard for me to see the light
My favorite time of day is night.
Because when the sun is brightly shining
I hide my tears and mute my whining.
But at night its hard for others to see
The pain and hurt inside of me.
For my body is not as tired as my soul.
And I wonder, "How I will accomplish my goal?"
At night it's safe to express my fear and doubt
By lying down in my bed without standing out.
I imagine that I've had a dynamic day.
Although so many obstacles are still in my way.
While I wonder if I have done my best
The moon gives me permission to rest.
Soon I will reach that special place
But first I have some fears to face.
Fears that are inside of me.
Fears that are not always easy to see.
I know that this phase is only a test
And I must complete my chosen quest.
Facing trial and error in the broad day light.
Then expressing my fears as I lay at night.

Waking Up

Lord,
Thank you for waking me up this morning
and starting me on my way.
Thank you for showing me more of you each day.
Thank you for managing this beautiful earth
Where everyday is a gift just as the day of my birth.
For every second that you bless me to see
Tells me that you have more plans for me.

Are You Sure?

Are you sure, Lord?
Are you sure about me?
Am I supposed to take literally
the visions that I see?
Is my mind supposed to believe
The things that I am chosen to receive?
I mean no disrespect.
I just want to double check.
If you are sure
that you can make my heart and mind pure.
For so long I have been ashamed.
I thought that my struggles were a game.
And that I was the blame.
But you allowed my hard times to happen
for your greater good,
While my instabilities were misunderstood.
But now that I am stable
I know that you are able
And that the vision I saw was not a fable.
What I saw was so great
I thought that you made a cosmic mistake.
And that this place was not chosen for me.
Because I could not handle the thought of victory.

For a long time I have been down.
With a lot of negative people around.
And I started to think so lowly of myself
That I couldn't fathom a life of wealth and good health.
And even though this world may be full of coldness
With your help I can face it with boldness.
And work my assignment with the strength to endure
Because you have chosen me for this
and you are absolutely sure.

This poem is dedicated to my brother Michael.

My Dreams

My dreams are real
And my heart can feel
That time will reveal
What the world can't steal.

 Gifts

Our gifts are meant to edify one another
And to unify each other as sister and brother.
We must understand
The higher purpose and plan.
Together we can conquer the darkest beast
Once our gifts and inner powers are released.
The chaos will cease
as we work towards peace.
We all have contributions to give
And a better life to live.
So please find what your purpose is about
So that the rest of the world won't be left out.

A Secret to Success

There is something that you owe yourself.
If you want good health and a life full of wealth.
God has some major plans for you
But you have some inner work to do.
Because there is a reason why your dreams don't last.
It's because you've been holding on to your past.
It eats away at your success.
This anger and pain that was repressed.
I know how that person put trauma on you.
And acted as if there's only drama on you.
But only you are carrying this heavy load
While they barely even remember that episode.
They may have tested you or rejected you
And you want to hold on to a grudge
like the rest would do.
But you must let go.
Because you will not be able to grow.
There may be so many years wasted before you realize
That you were spiritually paralyzed.
All those projects you started that never got finished
Was because a piece of your soul was diminished.
But when you let go, you will be replenished.
You must release the pain that you went through
And break those chains that are binding you.

This same release has happened to me
and it feels so good to live so free!
Your true purpose in life will come and find you
once you have the courage
to leave your past behind you.
It doesn't matter if the tears
have been flowing for many years.
Even strangers can identify who you are
Because of how soon you show them your scar.
You are in denial because you think you are fine
When in reality you are living in past time.
Your pain can be conquered with power of love
Because you have help from up above.
Whether you were shot, abused or even molested.
What's done is done. Now only you can accept it.
It may be hard to believe, but after a while,
they may decide to reconcile.
But if they are still rejecting, you can't stop.
Because jaws will drop once you make it to the top.
But first it has to be in your heart to forgive.
Then a prosperous life you are sure to live.
And this fortune that I am talking about,
You will possess both inside and out.
And your bright future will prove the rest,
once you apply to your life this secret to success.

Forgiveness Is

In order to live
We must forgive.
Forgiving is seeing the purpose
Behind surface.
Knowing that what seems scary
Is oftentimes necessary.
Although the pain hurts and your heart may cry.
You must search for that reason why.
Figure out why that challenge was chosen for you.
Follow the light to your break through.
Let it be clearly understood
That the struggle was designed for your greater good.
Then take your soul through the much needed repairs.
Freeing yourself from heavy burdens and cares.
For when a trial has successfully made you stronger,
you do not have to endure that pain much longer.
Though you may move on to greater tests
you will achieve your spiritual best.
Remembering that the lightest way to live
is to respect your test and thankfully forgive.

Being Successful

Sometimes being successful
is just simply living
by loving, caring, sharing and giving.

Sometimes being successful
is just being content
knowing that your life was heaven sent.

Sometimes being successful
is working your God given plan
even if it is not approved by man.

Sometimes being successful
is ignoring the concept of success.
Because to be alive is to truly be blessed.

Moving On

At times when I am afraid and all alone
I want to go back to my comfort zone.
That's when I need more courage to search and roam
Because I still have not found my home.
I desire to reach a time and place
Where I can thrive in my chosen space.
But when my past and future plays tug-of-war
I tend to lose track of what I am searching for.
That's when I wonder if there will always be
a sense of uncertainty inside of me.
I ask, "Could this be the purpose of trust,
to not know my outcome yet go on I must?"
I have to keep moving. I cannot stay in this spot.
Because this life of mine is all that I've got.
I know where I've been and I want to see more.
So I'll just have to walk toward that unopened door.

My Epiphany

It got to the point where I couldn't help but see
that there was something wrong with me.
Before now, I was in so much denial
that I would put everyone else on trial.
I'd say, "He has a problem and so does she.
and the whole world is taking things out in me!"
I would live my life day after day
disregarding what others would try and say
about me and my problem.
To me the ones who've tried to give me a hand
were only more people who did not understand.
I didn't know that their criticism
was out of care and concern.
So when they stretched out to reach me,
they would just get burned.
Burned by the fire that was consuming me.
Burned by my problem that I couldn't see.
I was full of so much stress and strife.
They would cut me off just to save their own life.
But I didn't get it because I didn't know.
So, I let a lot of valuable people go.
When they would walk away, I would just say, "Bye!"
Not knowing that my problem was the reason why.

And as my problem grew taller,
my circles were much smaller.
Until it just got to the point where I couldn't help but see
that there was something wrong with me.
And it was really a close call.
Because I began to think that I didn't need people at all.
Until I reached a place on my journey to success
where I'd have to turn around or face my mess.
Face my problem that others were talking about.
My problem that I could no longer doubt.
A problem that when I finally saw it,
I was in so much awe of it.
It was hideous and it was huge. It had such a magnitude
I just knew it was affecting my attitude.
It was painful to see it.
And it hurt even more to be it.
Immediately I said,
"It's no wonder why the people don't call!
It's no wonder why I started to fall."
I went from mad to sad. From sad to glad.
I started thinking about the relationships that I had.
I thought about all of the people that walked away.
And how their absence contributed
to my epiphany today.

My Epiphany cont'd

And if I saw them again, all I would say is,
"Thank you for showing me that people deserve more.
And I don't blame you for walking out of that door."
And for the few people that didn't give up.
Although it was rough you've had more than enough.
Your love saved my life, you saved the day.
You inspired me to improve my way.
And as my hopes and dreams come true.
It would be an honor to share them with you.
Still I am faced with the reality
that identifying my problem is just a part of the strategy.
But half of my battle is already won.
And I know that I will overcome.
Because it got to the point
where I couldn't help but see
that there was something wrong with me.

Eye Of My Storm

My storm is not over. I'm only standing in the eye.
I have to brace myself before the rest passes by.
I cannot come out of the shelter. I must stay inside.
Although the sun is still shining I still have to hide.
Because my storm is not over. It's only taking a break.
And it's too early to know
how much damage it will make.
It will seem like two storms although I know it's only one.
And I'll have to remember that
when the rest of it comes.
In life it seems like certain problems are new.
When the old ones are still just passing through.
I feel the beating rain and I hear the fierce wind.
Yet I know that my storm will eventually end.

Calming Down

I used to be busy but I was not productive.
I wanted to build but I was not constructive.
I would see my target but would miss my aim.
Then I realized that my burdens were the blame.
The day that piece of straw broke the camel's back.
The day I had a severe anxiety attack.
The day that forced me to get my mind on track.
So I agreed to live in a psych ward for a week.
To relax and listen to the experts speak.
They assessed my situation and this was the bottom line
They said, "You're a talented girl and you'll be just fine.
Just live your life one day at a time."
But that was the biggest challenge for me.
After realizing the potential of what I could be
my future was all that my heart could see,
but not worrying about tomorrow has set me free.
My mental slate became organized and clean.
My calming down and starting over, felt like a dream.
It was as if I had a second chance at life.
And God reduced my stress and eliminated my strife.
Although I trust and hope that my future is swell
I can let go of the stress because only time will tell.

Conscience

I have no choice
but to listen to my inner voice.
This whisper inside of me can not be ignored.
It is something to be adored.
When there is no trusted advisor around.
There is inner guidance to be found.
As I focus closely I find
That my solutions are in the quiet thoughts of my mind.
I used to experience self doubt a bit
And just talk myself right out of it.
Then later on I would regretfully say,
"I should've went with the answer that came my way."
Following my inner compass keeps me on the road.
Without carrying such a heavy load.
Listening to this voice has set me free.
And it will not be taken away from me.

Since I Became Conscious

There was a time in my life when I could only see
the things that would just revolve around me.
I'd think, "How complicated can this world be?"
Until one day the truth came and set me free.
The day that I became *conscious*.
And every since my mind has been enlightened.
My vital signs and senses
have also become heightened.
Now when I watch TV,
subliminal messages are obvious to me.
I hear concealed phrases that aren't blatantly said.
And I see how the masses are influenced and lead.
I feel a new found passion inside of my heart.
With a deeper love for people that sets me apart.
I can smell hatred and corruption from a mile away.
The odor reeks in the environment day after day.
Thankfully the taste of love is so divine,
that I was instantly addicted. It must always be mine.
Since I became conscious, my priorities have rearranged.
Even my taste in men has changed.
At first he had to earn so many amount of dollars.
He had to associate with the wealthy
and rich white collars.

His car had to be brand spanking new.
And he had to be impressed with my fake hairdo.
But those were the days when I didn't have a clue.
And now that my heart and mind are more free
I can really get what is in store for me.
I'm appreciating various manifestations of wealth.
And above all, is the value of knowing God
and myself.
Since I became conscious
Some people think that I'm **out there**.
They are absolutely right! That's why I don't care.
And I don't plan on going anywhere.
I'm not moving backwards. I'm only moving ahead.
I'm purifying myself from the destruction I was fed.
And it was hard to admit that I was being misled.
Many are called to this truth but few are selected.
I think it's because so many people reject it.
You must be ready in case this truth is brought to you.
If you're not open then it cannot be taught to you.
If this truth is something that you are blessed to see
then hear this poem again
to see how different it will be.
So you can gain a better understanding of me
and why I've changed
since I became
conscious.

Judgment

If we are free to live however we may...
If we are directly affected by what we do and say...
If rewards or retributions can come our way...
Is everyday a judgment day?

Temple

My body is a temple
And it is just that simple.
It houses God's Holy Spirit that dwells there.
So I have to administer to it special care.
It is my physical shell.
It's how I see, hear, feel, taste and smell.
The more that my body is nourished
The more that I am free to flourish.
On earth I have a lot of work to do.
And my body must last until I'm through.
Before, I did not initiate my care giving role.
Because I thought it was totally out of my control.
When I used to view life in reverse,
Thinking that my body would break down first.
But I realize that, for now, I need it.
So I am careful with how I treat and feed it.
It could be more complicated but for me it's simple.
There is light inside of my God given temple.

God

Through the gospel of Jesus
God has been my guide.
His presence was all around me
But I had to let him inside.

Discovery

I started to search through my mind
because I wanted to see what I would find.
Knowing that my intellect was healthy and strong
I ventured inside to see where I belong.
And today I am at peace because I have found it.
A place where I'll rest now that I am grounded.
I am no longer a pilgrim exploring my own inner land,
but now a citizen in a world that I am starting to understand.
Although I've found this place I am not through.
For I have some building and growing to do.
That's why I cherish this ground where I am now planted.
My inner territory must not be taken for granted.
Because I crossed my personal deserts and seas,
just to find a place to be at ease.
The exclusive journey is not just for me,
but also for all humanity.
A world of peace can be found from anywhere.
Just search inside and you'll be there.
Because I knew who the world wanted me to be.
But I customized my life to represent me.
I look forward to a life of prosperity and wealth.
Because I have found God and I am learning myself.

Like Me

I would try to convince people
to agree with my thoughts.
I wanted them to purchase
the same items that I bought.
I wanted people to practice the things I believed.
I wanted others to appreciate the insight I received.
I was controlling before I realized
That my life was being customized.
Soul searching became a game of hide and seek
Because I didn't see how my differences
made me unique.
But today I am free because now I know
That my high is my high and my low is my low.
My dreams are about who I want to be.
And I imagine the things that I want to see.
I understand that a song in which I find inspiration
Can cause another to change the radio station.
We all don't enjoy eating the same type of food.
We even express differently the same kind of mood.
The clothes we wear and what we watch on TV
Are more elements of our individuality.
Attempts to change people was bad for my health
Because I lacked courage to be myself.
I used to find my preferences frustrating and confusing.
But I appreciate them now and I find them amusing.
I cannot force things on people I can only share
If they are open and if they care.
Embracing differences in others have set me free.
So I no longer try to convince people to live like me.

Light Night

When times are so hard and rough
some people give up on the positive stuff.
Deciding that enough is enough
and that embracing the darkness
means that they're tough.
And a part of them thinks that our optimism is strange,
because they don't believe
that the bad things can change.
When they are immersed in a fear and a hate.
they see our trust and love and can't relate.
But they too can be gifted with this special sight
that allows them to see this light.
Because even though we keep our shine together,
we still can see the trouble.
And although we have our hope and faith,
we still can relate to the struggle.
We still keep a lot of people around
knowing that they could let us down.
It's all good,
because respected enemies are our friends
because they are a helpful means to an end.
Even when things are out of place
we manage to keep a smile on our face.
Although the night may seem cold and scary
We know it's for a purpose that's temporary.

The Place To Be

Welcome… to this world. This is a private space.
This is an exclusive place.
There are so many loving others here
that there is nothing for you to fear.
When you step into this light
everything is alright
and there is not a problem in sight.
Only solutions that we haven't implemented yet.
In this world, there are no regrets.
Only situations that we haven't learned from yet.
Over here we make no spiritual judgments.
We just see others that we don't understand yet.
So just take your shoes off.
And take your blues off.
Simply come in and relax
because you are no longer under attack.
Over here, you don't have to watch your back.
There is no need to.
Because the only person that can emotionally hurt you,
is you.
So just guard your own heart
although we won't try to take it.
Hold it close because only you can break it.
By handing it over to someone else
and never learning to love God and yourself.

In this world, love is your only invitation
And you don't have to make any reservations.
Come here anytime while loving you
So you can understand what and why we do.
Appreciating the constructive words that we say
And why we choose to live our lives this way.
This is an experience you can't afford to miss
Because you have to see that this place exists.
This paradise is real.
And all that you have to do is heal.
conquer your fears so you can start to feel.
Feel them, feel you and even feel me
Because this is the place to be.
Do you know
That there is joy and peace right here on this earth?
For renewing your mind is the greatest rebirth.
Do you know
That you don't have to wait until the next life
To be free from your fears, hatred and strife?
You can enjoy your life right here and right now.
and if you don't know how
Just ask yourself why can't you relate.
Start soul searching with no need to hesitate.
Beginning with only a thought in your mind
about this place that is possible to find.

The Place To Be cont'd

This world is not a fantasy. It is a reality.
Just renew your mind and elevate your mentality.
It is simply a matter of making a decision
Though this is not a club, cult or religion.
This is God's world and it's up to you to see
That this is really the place to be.

The Sky Is Not The Limit!

The sky is high this we know.
Still there are no limits to where we can go.
So even if your goal seems so far away.
You are closer to reaching it day after day.
And as you go higher things might seem strange
Because the atmosphere was designed to change.
But with a positive mentality you'll get things done
And you'll conquer your fears just for fun.

Part Two:
Enlightened Love

Enlightened Love by Alicea Crafte

This painting symbolizes one moving out of the darkness of fear into the light of trust.

I Can Feel

I was hurt as a child and even as an adult.
So a cold-hearted woman was the result.
I couldn't accept pleasure
for trying to block out the pain.
My sense of compassion was going down the drain.
So when a man would approach me
and try to come close.
I would treat him as if he were a ghost.
His presence was hazy because my mind was unclear.
His sweet words were sounds
that my heart wouldn't hear.
His qualities I didn't appreciate or receive
Because to me, they were only make believe.
Then one day,
After I let some good people slip away.
I lifted my head to say,
"I cannot live my life this way!"
And this new light that I was seeing.
Made me a more constructive being.
So I took my heart and I did the unthinkable.
I wanted to test if love was truly unsinkable.
I unthawed my heart that was cold and numb.
and warmed it up for a special someone.
It actually felt good.
And this trust thing was being more understood.
The warm tears from my eyes were a blessing so real.
Because it they were the evidence that once again,
I can feel.

This poem is dedicated to my sweetheart Benjamin Davis

May I love you?

May I love you?
I mean the way that I want to?
Because I want to love you without any fear
As if I have never cried a tear.
I want to say things to you that most are afraid to say
Because expressing my love will make my day.
Today, I am not scared
I am fully prepared.
I want to give to you
Just because...I want to.
And that is reason enough when the love is true.
Especially when I love you.
Baby when I love you, I'll love you
from wherever you are.
Just ask, how close is a shining star?
Answer is, it's close enough.
Close enough to shine on us when times get rough.
So no matter where in this world you might be
You will always see love coming from me.
Because I can twinkle like a star in your darkest night.
Or shine like the sun even when it's light.
But I want to know if that's alright.
And I know that it seems like I'm asking
But I'm loving you already and it's everlasting.

So you don't have to answer
because this love has begun.
I'm only asking right now just for fun.
May I love you?
Because this thing is more than make believe
And I trust that you have the courage to receive.
I can't help but love you because I'm trusting me
And I know this is how things are supposed to be.
I'm telling you that this is how I live
And I won't be myself if I'm afraid to give.
So do you want me to or not?
Should I give you all that I've got?
With no hesitation …
With no expectation …
And more importantly, with no expiration?
So not only can I love you
I already do.
Though I can't help but ask…
May I love you?

Not To Love

See, that's why I decided not to love you
And to leave your memory behind.
Because it's torture just to have you dwelling in my mind.
So I know that if I let you in my heart
My world would only break apart.
Things get broken when they are not handled properly.
That's what you did with my heart, my sacred property.
So why give my love to someone who doesn't care.
Why take my heart through unnecessary repairs.
If it's not broken, then don't break it.
If my heart is not yours then don't try to take it.
You know I care about you, I won't try to fake it.
But deep down I know that we won't make it.
Even if we make up.
I know we'll eventually forever break up.
Because I realize through our much needed space
That my heart must reside in a safer place.
At least I have learned my lesson this time.
I'll share my love but my heart is mine.
And that's why I decided not to love you.
I'm working hard to leave all those smiles behind.
Because it is torture to have you dwelling in my mind.
So, I know that if I let you in my heart
That my world would only break apart.

I have sense enough to know
That this has gone as far as it should go.
Because when I take a look at where we are.
I realize that we haven't gone far.
And it's a shame because
we would have been really good friends
But I did not let other feelings come in.
Those feeling that were so deceiving
That I prematurely starting believing
That it was your love I would be receiving.
Luckily for my heart and me,
I'm secure enough to set you free.
So even though I care, I won't attempt to reach you.
I've learned from my mistakes
but I won't attempt to teach you.
So if you don't believe that your partner is me,
Then I'll have to move on and just let it be.
That's why I decided not to love you.
I'm leaving all those good times behind.
Because it's torture just to have you in mind.
It's so obvious that if I let you in my heart
That my world would only break apart.
That's why I decided not to love you.
But the irony is, I already do.
Why else would I be writing this poem about you.

Bad Mouth

Ladies I just don't understand.
Why do you pick up the phone to call your friends
Just to bad moth your man?
Don't you still need him?
Won't you still sex and feed him?
Do you think your friends actually believe
That you are tired enough to leave.
You two are staying together and that's why you complain.
And this back and forth is only driving you insane.
Why gossip on the phone
When you are not ready to leave him alone?
Because even though your stories are sad.
It is yourselves that you make look bad.
Because you might have reasons to walk away.
After you cry, you choose to stay.
And that's okay.
But the main reason why your friends may lend an ear
Is because your drama is so entertaining to hear.
You'll soon forget about all of that emotional harm.
By the end of the week, you'll be back in his arms.
So I really don't understand
Why would you bad mouth your man.
Since you are not ready to give him the boot.
It is best to keep your problems on mute.

Your friends don't need to be updated
Because when your man comes around them,
he'll sense that he's hated.
He'll wonder how could those words leave your mouth
When your communication with him is headed south.
So no matter how much your friends may want to pry
And wonder if he makes you cry.
Just make the best of it.
And quietly work through the rest of it.
I am one who strongly believes
That there is no use of complaining
if you aren't willing to leave.
So do your relationship a favor.
Don't entertain them
By bad mouthing him.

Meant To Be

I am not feeling this potential relationship.
I am really not feeling this.
In the beginning should be an ignorant bliss.
Yet our infatuation phase was a hit and miss.
You being a decent man doesn't make you mine.
And I refuse to waste my precious time.
Today, days are weeks and weeks are years.
So why should I force myself to stay right here.
This thing is not meant to be
When it is draining all of my energy.
I want to build up and you want to tear down
And I will not search through love's lost and found.
Although the time we spent was short and brief.
I can already see that you will cause me some grief.
I became familiar with your kind.
When I fast forwarded to our future then pressed rewind
Because what I saw made me say, "Never Mind."
The timing may not be right for you.
But it could be perfect for somebody new.
Right now a worthy prospect is starting to pray.
Let's listen in close to what he has to say.

"Lord let her be strong. Let her be wise.
Let me see the light when I look into her eyes.
Let her be virtuous, strong and fine.
I promise to be a better man this time.
And, my lady, if you can hear me,
whether you are near or far.
I will be brought to wherever you are."
So I cannot stay here in the wrong person's face.
I need to clean out my personal space.
I am not about to give you my precious heart
Nor become the horse that pulls your cart.
You want to use your promises as a dangling bait
And hope that I am foolish enough to wait.
But this opportunity is not for me
Because it doesn't take wasted years for me to see
That we were just not meant to be.

I'm Learning Him

I'm learning him from the inside out
I want to know without a doubt
what this man is all about.
Now, even though I have a school girl crush
This is a process that cannot be rushed
Because if I'm impatient
his intentions would be hushed.
I'm only opened to that man
who'll give me the love that I deserve.
So even though I'm feeling him,
I'll just sit back and observe.
I want to know how he carries his wit and his charm,
and if he's holding someone in his masculine arms.
I wish to learn about his inspirations and plans
And how he works with his mind and talented hands.
Then when I find out what he intends to do.
I'll wonder if he is the type that will follow through.
Is he my true companion indeed?
Does he have that mindset to protect and feed?
Is he the type to hold an ambitious woman back?
Or does he admire a woman
who can make her money stack?
Does he have the desire to control me?
Or does he respect me as a person equally?

What is his idea of strength and security?
Can I enjoy his spiritual maturity?
And even if my questions are based out of fear.
I'll use them to my advantage before I let him near.
These are things that I want to see.
They are qualities that are important to me.
I know that I am not asking for much
When it comes down to the person
that my soul will touch.
Before I attract what I want my essence
must be the same.
Otherwise my energy and character will be the blame.
If he's for me, I'll know by the smiles on my face.
And how my world will continue to be a warm place.
We'll have the freedom to push our inhibitions away.
While he's learning me as well and I'm making his day.
I trust that he is selective too.
For we must be careful in what we do.
We're learning each other not too fast or too slow.
Because we both have places that we want to go.
And no matter how much of him
I am privileged to explore
I know I can always learn about him some more.
Our lesson plan is coming along so far so good.
I know our connection is understood.
And only time will tell me if I'm hanging out on a limb.
Because today I'm taking a risk and I'm learning him.

Beauty

I don't know who other women may want to be
But my standard of beauty happens to be me.
I'm not comparing myself to those chicks on TV.
What's the point? When I can look at me!
I look within to see that beauty is mine.
So how dare society attempt to define.
With darker? Lighter?
Wronger? Righter?
This or that?
Thin? Fat?
Sheer perfection? Or a genetic mistake?
Please give me a break!
I wish that the women would stop
competing and comparing
And realize that the men will never stop staring.
They will always stare at her, me and you.
So just be yourself and do what you want to do.
There is only one person that I want to be.
Because my standard of beauty will always be me.

Emotions

Are our emotions illusions
That we perceive to be real?
Are we conditioned to create
the way that we feel?

Relationships

Relationships are to be enjoyed.
Not taken for granted or destroyed.
Because people do not have to be near us.
They could distance themselves if they dislike or fear us.
It is a compliment to your energy and essence.
If a person choose to be in your presence.
So handle them with care and treat them good.
Let your appreciation for them be understood.
Whether they are familiar to you
or if they are a stranger
Their well being should not be in danger.
For to hurt others is to hurt yourself.
Respecting people is good for your spiritual health.
The world does not have to be lonely or cold
When there are people around with hands to hold.
There is warm and loving place to be found.
When you value the people who are near and around.

This poem is dedicated to my entire family.
Hi Layna!

Part Three:
Barriers Broken

Barriers Broken by Alicea Crafter

his painting represents people appreciating differences in
·thers.

Grateful

This message is for all of the whites.
Who've always had the desire to love and unite.
You were the ones who had our backs
and did not prejudge us because we were black.
You are more than an exception
To all that hatred and rejection.
You were our trusted ally.
When we needed help to get by.
You were against all the suffering that we went through.
Although we were the victims, you cried too.
And we are so grateful
for you not being hateful.
In a time where prejudice is still tried and true.
We have to give credit to whom honor is due.
Today, when I needed a job to pay my bills
You didn't focus on my color
but you admired my skills.
Yesterday, when we marched,
I know you took pride.
As we protested for civil rights
you were right by our side.
And the day before, when the slaves hid underground.
My family took shelter in your home,
Though you pretended that they were not around.
And we are so grateful
for you not being hateful.
Especially in those times
when loving us was a crime.

You risked your own kindred's respect and trust
All in the name of helping us.
As we celebrated emancipation,
you were dancing and drinking
Instead of questioning, "What Lincoln was thinking?"
It is amazing through all the pain and insanity
How you managed to keep your love
and humanity.
You let your children play with us.
You came to church to pray with us.
It is nice to see you more than once in a while
When you genuinely greet us
with your welcoming smile.
Even though there is still room to grow.
We appreciate you and we want you to know.
That we still need you.
Uniting humanity is what we can do.
I see you, my friend.
Making it easier as our struggle
comes close to an end.
The truth is,
There are still some inequalities out there.
But we know better than to think that you do not care.
And we are just so grateful
For you not being hateful.
Thank you.

Unite and Conquer
(evolved)

A nation that is divided will fall.
So we all must come together to build up a wall.
As long as there is hatred between white and black.
We're all vulnerable to this country being attacked.
White and black...Black and white.
Will we finally get this thing right?
Notice that what I am saying may pertain to you
Whether you look brown, yellow, red or blue.
Because although there is more to us
than a shade or color.
This racial epidemic
affects the way we view one another.
Day after day, I am more convinced
That racism is only a symptom
of what we're up against.
We are challenging the spirit of fear.
And only love can make it disappear.
Oh yes, fear was the engrained seed
That brought forth hatred, discrimination and greed.
And now more love is all that we need.
It's in the best interest of this land being free
That we must invest in a greater bond
between you and me.

Will the division come to an end
we challenge where this outlook began?
Achieving unity requires trust and bravery
to question if we're all negatively affected
by war and slavery.
I'm just searching for the light to leave hatred behind.
I know that changing laws will not change the heart
and the mind.
Has the past made you fearful too?
Are hurtful views embedded inside of you?
Do you trust that the stereotypes are true?
Or is your heart yearning for something new?
The fear of differences, our hearts must fight it
so all the citizens in this land can be united.
The fact that this country is now diverse
Must be accepted and not be reversed.
We are all connected.
We are all affected.
And everyone must be respected.
We have dominion over the earth's food chain.
So why cause a fellow human being hurt and pain.
When you explore the galaxies in outer space
You'll find that we must survive in this place.
So why judge another because of their race,
you love the image that is on your face?
is unity that will keep this country strong.
So we all must feel that we belong.

Unite and Conquer cont'd

This is not a one sided quest for unity.
We must build up the mindsets in every community.
Challenging us all to face and conquer our past.
Or is that too much for me to ask?

Freedom's Burden

eedom?...You want to know about freedom?
'ell, being free
not as easy as I thought it would be.
fact, being free has become a burden
at is so full of pain.
ecause now I see the people wearing invisible chains.
nd these mental chains are not an illusion.
et I refuse to accept a negative conclusion.
am traveling this journey that is freeing my mind
nd I don't want to leave the people behind.
was in mental bondage
nd it was hard breaking through.
, I understand why freedom
ay be intimidating to you.
ut delivering others from mental oppression
as become my obsession.
etting people to think and move
a more positive direction.
ecause I know that our problems will not always last.
ee a bright future coming from our dark past.
ut it's a burden to be free
ecause it's my responsibility
help the people to see who they can potentially be.
can't enjoy this freedom selfishly.

Freedom's Burden cont'd

The need for mental freedom is often misunderstood.
That's why outsiders focus on the surface
of broken neighborhoods.
Certain charities and some celebrities
want to lend a helping hand.
But at times it seems that most don't understand
Why many urban communities are poor on this land.
Their heart felt donations may not produce lasting fruit
If we don't pluck the ghetto's problems
up from their roots.
So boarding up abandoned houses and
building playgrounds is not all it's about.
When the ghetto needs a makeover
from the inside out.
Don't get me wrong. Good intentions are fine.
But efforts may be in vain
if we are not freeing urban minds.
If we don't put this mental struggle to an end
the cleaned up ghettos might get messed up again.
It's not just the time for that bucket of paint and soap.
If you want to make a difference
also give these children some hope.
Say to them, "Young man, no matter your mistakes
You come from greatness and that makes you great."
Tell that young sister, "Your natural beauty is fine.
But give your soul permission to shine."

We must educate our youth on our economic power
and how we can upgrade our own community
with our own dollars.
Let them know that they can achieve material success
and still be mentally oppressed.
Besides what is the purpose behind building wealth,
if you've never had the luxury of being yourself?"
Because our people are unique!
And when we smother that truth
It lowers the self esteem of our developing youth.
They appear to express rebellion rather than pride
When society suppresses who they are inside.
It seems that our youth are confused
About who they are supposed to be.
As a people are we even culturally free?
Or is oppression still festering in our community?
Are we influenced to endure an identity removal
That may train us to seek society's approval?
Are these insecurities misunderstood?
When the focus is on the surface
of low income neighborhoods?
If we are still defining who we are
After that's established we can really go far.
So I use my voice as a contribution
Hoping that together we will implement the greatest solution.
Although this outlook is obvious for me to see.
People have to decide who they want to be.
And if what I'm saying makes sense to you.
Then imagine all the building that we could do.

Freedom's Burden cont'd

Although people have been spreading this message for years.
Hopefully this time around it is loud and clear.
The ignorance was bliss.
But now I can't let go of this.
This freedom is a burden that I bare
And if more people will take their fair share.
It would be a better world out there.

February

eople why do we think that it's scary
o talk about our history when it's not February.
ke all of a sudden we become aware
f a history that is always there.
 February, we remember about that dream
om the honorable Dr. King.
nd in February it's,
ft every voice and sing
l' earth and heaven ring.
ut by March the 1st,
 hink it's a shame.
ow our lives and our progress may still be the same.
as our culture been reduced
o a holiday and a game?
ur story has the power to build up other races.
nce we rise up from stereotypical places
nd start appreciating the beauty
f our own minds and faces.
nd somebody please tell me why...
Vhy do we only light firecrackers on the 4th of July?
Vhen 1776 was not our year of independence.
 at year we were not free.
Ve were still in slavery.
o while we're standing over that barbecue grill.
nd putting ribs in our mouths, let's just keep it real.

While they were talking about
how the stars were spangled,
Our people were in captivity still being strangled.
So let's honor January 1st of 1865.
The day emancipation helped our people to survive.
Because the only thing to me that seems to be scary.
Is that we're proud to be ourselves in February.

Black On Purpose
(evolved)

used to question what was my life about
but now without a shadow of a doubt.
know so many reasons why I am here.
and why I don't have to live my life in fear.
m talking about reasons that caused me
to break out of confinement.
to get busy on my divine assignment.
but 1st, I had to search beneath the surface
to see that God created me black on purpose.
his is all about me being black
because my cultural esteem was once under attack.
hey say that the label black may be culturally outdated.
because it's connected to a past
where our colors were separated.
I still use it to get my point across.
so that our sense of identity will not be lost.
understand that our character
not determined by the color of our skin.
know that we are all connected
by the light that shines within.
but I am still black on purpose.
and as much as I appreciate everyone else.
have to take this moment to celebrate myself.
because I could have been born into any other race.
could be wearing an entirely different face.
but I'm black!
here are no coincidences when it comes down to me.
even the year I was born was a part of my destiny.

Because of my strong optimistic ways
I am a part of these changing days.
This is the era in which I am placed.
And my contributions cannot be erased.
Because I am here on purpose.
And I can't hide myself any longer.
When my struggles have made me stronger.
The more I see, the more I realize
That my hair and my skin are a symbol and a prize.
I remind the world of a battle that humanity won.
And how we were victorious over slavery
centuries before it begun.
Because God allowed that on purpose too.
American slavery taught the world that,
Chains can be forced on your body and mind.
And freedom may seem impossible to find.
But when you trust in the Lord
and work towards a better day
You can make your struggles go away!
I know that God made me black on purpose.
And this thing, goes way beneath the surface.
God made you on purpose too.
So let's unleash our greatness
and see what we can do.
I know that God made me black on purpose.

Women Like Me

am sick and tired of this mess!
Waiting for reparations that still need to be addressed.
his is not about 40 acres and a mule.
m not holding my breath, I'm not a fool.
know that this world can be cruel.
his is about the men in our own community
who have not given back.
o the women who've endured
while their minds are off track.
Women who've stood by our men
nce that shipment arrival.
Women who've dedicated their lives
o our people's survival.
nd I take this reparations thing personally.
ecause I'm speaking up for women like me.
Je were ripped from your arms but we stayed.
hey tried to break us down but we prayed.
o we can still be a family but you've strayed.
have respect and appreciation for diversity.
ut let's face the fears between you and me.
oday, not enough husbands and fathers
re in our homes.
Women are having to make it on their own.
's like our future together is almost gone.

Women Like Me cont'd

Yet I have faith that somewhere out there
That there are more men in this community
who know and care.
After our grandparents tore down the walls of segregation.
Our people scattered in a massive separation.
Though gaining the freedom of integration
was necessary for our progress.
We've seemed to have lost our sense of unity
throughout the process.
As we strive to get our community under control.
We need to take pride in our privileged roles.
When love and trust was no where around.
The family unit is where strength
and motivation was found.
That's why I take this reparations thing personally
Because I'm speaking up for women like me.
I'm not speaking up for those
who are full of bitterness and resentment.
But for us women
who are sticking by our historic commitment.
Women like me.
And I'm not speaking up for those
who don't understand
The challenges that we've conquered
while here on this land.
But for us women who build with a loving hand.

omen like me.
n not speaking up for those
ho buy that nice house and car.
nen all of a sudden forget how valuable you are.
ut for us women who remember that you are a star.
omen like me.
n proudly representing the women
om our story's beginning.
ho weren't this close to our happy ending.
ho passed on this message
nat right now I am sending.
Women hold on. Men come home.
omen hold on. Men come home."
ease understand that life is not only about you.
ake a look at the timeline
nd what we are going through.
e need you now more than ever without a doubt
ecause our community is facing a potential burnout.
o we apologize if we come across rude.
e apologize if we offend you with our attitude.
e will even control our snappy temper.
nough it's not easy working with heroes
ho don't seem to remember.
emember that we have a greater job to do.
emember that we are somebody's ancestors too.
emember to appreciate the women
ho are connected you.
ecause together our community will make it through.

Women Like Me cont'd

I trust that this historic compensation
Is not just a figment of my imagination.
I view this relative situation
And only yearn for more participation.
As I look back at our efforts it breaks my heart
To think that our people will forever be torn apart.
And I'm taking this reparations thing personally.
Because I'm speaking up for women like me.

Triumphant Woman

Day by day I'm learning the magnitude
Of me being a triumphant woman
With a positive attitude.
Possessing the power and passion that promotes unity.
With love to give to the world and to my community.
Because I was fortunate enough to identify and dismiss
Subliminal problems that some don't realize exist.
And if what I've said so far, isn't making any sense,
Just let me inform you on what I was up against.
You see, I was taught to care,
As other people look and stare.
I was conditioned to be insecure
About revealing my African hair.
But I have learned to love my precious coils.
So, no more harsh chemicals, only natural oils.
And society told me,
That I might become another Negro whore.
Yet I am privileged to know I am so much more.
This woman isn't just for the bedroom
But also the living room, the dining room
And even out of the front door.
Because I am made with ambition! I am made to soar!

Triumphant Woman cont'd

And society told me,
"Your father doesn't care about you."
But they'd failed to tell me that he'd be triumphant too!
After all these years, I am blessed to see
We will always be a family.
I am a part of a dynamic legacy.
And society told me to just give up on our men.
Since the majority are either unemployed
or locked up in the pen.
But they didn't tell me
that our men are too strong for defeat.
And they didn't tell me
that our men would land on their feet.
It is their triumph that I admire and respect.
It is triumph that I am honored to project.
And back in slavery,
the mothers taught that the way to survive
was to obey the master to stay alive.
But it's a new day and I will teach them the truth.
Building up their self esteem in the days of their youth.
I'll teach them not to be mentally deaf or blind.
I'll show them our future
so that they won't be left behind.

recting them to where our people
e yearning to be.
nd when they are ready to lead,
ey will start to teach me.
nd when we put our community back together
ery other community will be even better.
e world needs our people and so do I.
e will stick together and reach the sky.
make a difference because I know the magnitude
me being a triumphant woman
th a positive attitude.

Alicea Crafter

Alicea Crafter is changing the world with o poem at a time. While achieving her childhood g of becoming a poet, her empowering lyrics ha touched well over half a million people and h numbers are rapidly growing. Born and raised Detroit, MI., Alicea is preparing to launch a proje that the whole world can experience.

We are excited about the release of her first bo of poetry entitled, The Sky Is NOT The Limit. Topics each segment will uplift and energize us all. Alicec project creatively expresses her passion for hum progress. This body of work exposes our inr capabilities to overcome any obstacle while inspiring us to embrace c unique individualities. She has a passion for empowering others and h work is bound for global exposure.

"Her talent goes beyond any cultural barriers," says Derrick Hartfie owner and producer of The GNTV Network. She is walking towards longtime dream of hers and only time will tell us how this story unfolds. Sk provides inspirational entertainment full of vibrancy and enlightenmer Alicea is destined to change this world with one poem at a time.

For booking information or to contact Alicea, write or call:

Alicea Crafter
c/o PriorityONE Publications
P.O. Box 725
Farmington, MI 48332
(248) 820-1313

Or visit on the World Wide Web at:
www.aliceacrafter.com
info@aliceacrafter.com

BOOK ORDER FORM

The Sky is **NOT** the Limit!
A Book of Empowering Poetry
By Alicea Crafter

Name _____

Address _____

City _____ **State** _____ **Zip** _____

Phone _____ **Fax** _____

Email _____

Quantity	
Price *(each)*	$14.99
Subtotal	
S & H *(each)*	$2.99
MI Tax 6%	
TOTAL	

METHOD OF PAYMENT:

❑ Check or Money Order (*Make payable to:* **PriorityONE Publications**)

❑ Visa   ❑ Master Card   ❑ American Express

Acct No. _____

Expiration Date (*mmyy*) _____

Signature _____

Mail your payment with this form to:
PriorityONE Publications
P. O. Box 725
Farmington, MI 48332
(800) 596-4490 – Toll Free
(313) 893-3359 – Southeast Michigan
URL: http://www.p1pubs.com
Email: info@p1pubs.com

Printed in the United States
125426LV00001B